ĦAĠAR QIM & MNAJDRA PREHISTORIC TEMPLES
Qrendi

KATYA STROUD

PHOTOGRAPHY
DANIEL CILIA

HERITAGE BOOKS
IN ASSOCIATION WITH
H Heritage Malta

HOW TO GET THERE

Quarries

Misqa Tanks

Ħagar Qim

Mnajdra

Visitor Centre

Congreve Memorial

Ħamrija Tower

Ras il-Ħamrija

GOZO

COMINO

MALTA

Ħagar Qim
Mnajdra

5 km   North

By *Public Transport*: Bus Numbers 38 and 138 from Valletta main bus terminus and stop near Visitor Centre
By *car*: Main road leading to Żurrieq/Qrendi and follow the signs. Ample parking available next to the Visitor Centre.
By *open-top sightseeing buses*: Stop near Visitor Centre.
For further information on public transport please consult www.dca.gov.mt
For further information on opening hours and entrance fees please consult www.heritgemalta.org

Malta Insight Heritage Guides Series No: 20
General Editor: Louis J. Scerri

Acknowledgements:
A thank you goes to MariaElena Zammit, Joanne Mallia, Reuben Grima, Daniel Cilia, Josian Bonello, Pierre Bonello, Nicholas Vella, John J. Borg, Joe P. Borg, Guy and Cikka, for helping with this guide book in their own individual ways.

Published by Heritage Books, a subsidiary of Midsea Books Ltd, Carmelites Street, Sta Venera SVR 1724, Malta
sales@midseabooks.com
www.midseabooks.com

Insight Heritage Guides is a series of books intended to give an insight into aspects and sites of Malta's rich heritage, culture, and traditions.

Produced by Mizzi Design & Graphic Services

Editorial Copyright © Heritage Books
Literary Copyright © Katya Stroud
Illustration credits: Unless otherwise stated all illustrations in this book are property of Daniel Cilia.; time-line (Heritage Malta); photos of Flora and Fauna (John J. Borg); plan of Visitor Centre (Heritage Malta); portrait of Jean Houel (Painting by François-André Vincent at the Musée des Beaux-Arts. Courtesy of Dottoressa Gringeri Pantano); portrait of Giovanni Francesco Abela (National Library of Malta)

First published 2010
ISBN: 978-99932-7-317-2

INTRODUCTION

The prehistoric temples of Ħaġar Qim and Mnajdra hold a special place in the visitor's heart. Their idyllic setting, the questions they raise and the awe they inspire have placed them on the itinerary of visitors to the Maltese islands since the 18th century.

Ħaġar Qim and Mnajdra have also gained considerable prominence in the public eye through the extensive press coverage of the collapses they sustained in the 1990s, the horrific act of vandalism on Mnajdra in 2001, and the much-debated protective shelters completed in 2009. But what is it about these sites that warrants such national and international attention, at times provoking emotional debate?

Ħaġar Qim and Mnajdra are found in the garigue landscape along the south-western coast of Malta, 2km from the village of Qrendi. Standing at the top of a ridge, with the ground sloping away on all sides, Ħaġar Qim must have always been a conspicuous landmark. Mnajdra Temples, visible from Ħaġar Qim, are found 500m downhill, above the southern cliffs. Both megalithic complexes were built between the 4th and 3rd millennia BC, placing them amongst the earliest monumental buildings of such sophistication in the whole world.

The value of these temples has been recognized by the United Nations Educational, Scientific and Cultural Organization (UNESCO). The 1972 UNESCO World Heritage Convention provides for the inscription of sites of outstanding significance in the World Heritage List. The Ġgantija Temples were inscribed on the List in 1980. In 1992, this inscription was extended to include the sites of Ħaġar Qim, Mnajdra, Skorba, Ta' Ħaġrat, and Tarxien. The inscription of the Maltese Megalithic Temples recognizes that they are "an outstanding example of a type of building or architectural or technological ensemble or landscape which illustrates a significant stage in human history."

In nominating Ħaġar Qim and Mnajdra as part of this inscription, the Government of Malta has committed itself to safeguard these sites for the enjoyment of present and future generations on behalf of the international community.

On a local scale these sites have additional significance. Their unique nature has made them synonymous with the Maltese Islands, and together with other Megalithic Temples, they have become a symbol of Maltese national identity. Soon after their excavation, Ħaġar Qim and Mnajdra became national icons appearing on Maltese stamps and currency. The first stamp bearing an image of the

	EARLY NEOLITHIC				LATE NEOLITHIC			
Ghar Dalam 5000 - 4300 BC	Grey Skorba 4500 - 4400 BC	Red Skorba 4400 - 4100 BC	Żebbuġ 4100 - 3700 BC	Mġarr 3800 - 3600 BC	Ġgantija 3600 - 3200 BC	Saflieni 3300 - 3000 BC	Tarxien 3150 - 2500 BC
First settlers from Sicily and introduction of mixed farming.		Ritual practices at Skorba.	First evidence of burial in rock-cut tombs		Construction of first megalithic temples.		Mysterious disappearance of the temple culture.

te: Phases are usually named after the site they were first found in.
wever, these sites may have been used across various phases.

TEMPLE PERIOD

Maltese 5 Euro cent coin showing a niche at Mnajdra Temples

Maltese stamp issued in 1926-27 depicting the South Temple at Mnajdra

The idyllic setting of Ħaġar Qim and Mnajdra

Maltese temples was issued in 1926-27 and it depicted the South Temple at Mnajdra. The free-standing altar at Ħaġar Qim also appeared on the first set of Maltese coinage issued in 1974. In 2007 the Maltese designs for the Euro coins were chosen following a national consultation. Amongst the three winning designs was one of the niches at Mnajdra South Temple which now appears on the Maltese 5, 2 and 1 Euro cent coins.

In addition, their exceptional character has also made them vital for the Maltese economy through cultural tourism. The Megalithic Temples are a key component in the promotion of the Maltese Islands as a distinctive holiday destination.

These monuments also have considerable educational as well as recreational value. With one of the highest population densities in the world, Malta has very limited availability of open spaces for recreation. However, the landscape around Ħaġar Qim and Mnajdra which has been designated as an archaeological park, provides an invaluable recreational space with considerable ecological, historical and aesthetic qualities. Being also an educational resource of great potential, these temples are utilised to illustrate the achievements of the Temple Culture, the prehistoric origins of human exploitation of the Maltese archipelago, the changing relationship between people and their environment, and the problems of sustainability in a small island context.

THE LANDSCAPE

At first glance, the landscape of Ħaġar Qim and Mnajdra may seem rather barren yet it offered all the resources necessary for a community to flourish here some 5,500 years ago. The very topography and geology of this landscape are still shaping the activities carried out here today.

Ħaġar Qim and Mnajdra Temples are found within the Magħlaq Fault system, formed by the movement between the continental plates of Africa and Europe. To its north, there are the high cliffs on which Mnajdra stands, while on its south, there is a coastal shelf that gives access to the sea.

As a result of this Fault, three of the five geological strata found on the Maltese islands outcrop in this area:
• **Globigerina Limestone**: Found close to Ħaġar Qim Temples, it was the only type of stone used in its construction;
• **Lower Coralline Limestone**: Found close to Mnajdra Temples. Mnajdra was constructed in both Lower Coralline and Globigerina Limestone. Globigerina was probably transported downhill from a nearby outcrop. It is interesting to note that Lower Coralline Limestone, heavier than Globigerina, was not transported uphill for the construction of Ħaġar Qim.
• **Upper Coralline Limestone**: Found beneath the coastal cliffs. This is the only location in the Maltese islands where Upper Coralline is found beneath Lower Coralline Limestone, because it was downthrown by the Maghlaq Fault.

The topography at Ħaġar Qim Temples changes from arable land to garigue

One of the coastal caves close to Ħaġar Qim and Mnajdra Temples

Mnajdra Temples are found close to the coastal shelf that gives access to the sea

The caves and coastal deposits within this fault have yielded large quantities of remains dating back to the Quaternary Period, which started around 2.6 million years ago. Excavations in the area by Thomas Abel Brimage Spratt in 1858 and by Andrew Leith Adams in 1861 led to the discovery of remains of dwarf elephants and other animals that lived here during the Pleistocene (Zammit Maempel, 1986, pp.291-292).

Ħaġar Qim Temples are unusual because they stand on the crest of a ridge, while most other temple sites, including Mnajdra, are found on the slopes below a hilltop. As a result, the main temple building at Ħaġar Qim appears to look out in all directions. Apart from the entrance in the main façade it has a number of other doorways giving access to different parts of the building, as well as an external niche. These elements are not common to other temple buildings and seem to be a direct result of the site's relationship with its landscape setting. Ħaġar Qim is also located at the boundary between garigue and agricultural land. This land was very probably exploited by the prehistoric farmers who built the temples.

Mnajdra Temples, on the other hand, are found below the ridge, located closer to the coastal shelf that gives access to the sea. As may be noted at other temple sites in Malta, nearby access to the sea and

to land suitable for agriculture played an important part in determining the location of these buildings, and Ħaġar Qim and Mnajdra appear to complement each other in providing access to both.

At the top of the hill, around 250m from Mnajdra are the Misqa Tanks. These are a group of large rock-cut water cisterns that collect clean rainwater from a rock outcrop. A supply of freshwater is a fundamental need for people and animals to survive and since this part of the island has relatively few springs, storage of winter rain is necessary to ensure a supply of water during the dry summer. It is not clear how old these tanks are, but they may even date back to prehistory.

The area of Ħaġar Qim and Mnajdra Temples has also seen considerable quarrying activity. Small pockets of rock-cutting can be seen in the landscape between the two temples and although evidence is

Aerial view of Misqa Tanks

Some of the rock-cut tanks at Misqa still retain water today

Congreve memorial

Tal-Ħamrija Tower

Filfla

limited, these may have been used in prehistory. The outcropping Lower Coralline Limestone in this part of the island has also led to extensive modern quarrying west of Mnajdra. These quarries were closed down in the early 1990s so as to safeguard the natural environment and landscape context of the prehistoric monuments and there are now plans to have these filled with inert waste.

The coastal shelf that provided access to the sea in prehistory was recognised as a risk in the 17th century, since it is also vulnerable to attack from the sea. The Knights of St John therefore built the Ħamrija Tower, one of thirteen coastal towers built during the reign of Grand Master De Redin. These towers were part of the Islands' defensive system, and were built to guard them from enemy landings and incursions.

Further along the coast is the Congreve Memorial commemorating General Sir Walter Norris Congreve, a decorated World War I General and Governor of Malta, who died in office in 1927. Congreve was buried at sea in the Channel between Malta and the islet of Filfla – the Congreve Channel.

The little island of Filfla, dominating the seaward view from the sites must have served as a useful landmark to mariners. There is no evidence to indicate that the island was ever inhabited but a chapel dedicated to the Assumption stood in a small cave from 1343 until it was destroyed in an earthquake in 1856.

The islet was used for target practice by British and NATO forces during the 20th century until 1970. It is now protected for its ecological value since being isolated from the mainland, Filfla has a unique eco-system and is home to several endemic species.

Flora and Fauna

Land cover here consists of steppic and garigue vegetation (*xagħri*). The flora is mainly that prevalent in the Mediterranean such as the Sea Squill (*Għansar - Urginea maritima*). Endemic species, found only in Malta, such as the Maltese Spurge (*Tengħud tax-Xagħri - Euphorbia melitensis*) and the Maltese Fleabane (*Tulliera ta' Malta - Chiladenus bocconei*) also grow here, whilst the sparse tree cover includes the Carob tree (*Siġra tal-ħarrub - Ceratonia siliqua*) and the Fig tree (*Siġra tat-tin - Ficus carica*).

Animal species are mainly represented by insects. However one may often come across the endemic Maltese Wall Lizard (*Gremxula ta' Malta – Podarcis filfolensis*) crossing the footpath that joins the two sites. The Weasel (*Ballottra - Mustela nivalis*)

may also occasionally be encountered here. Bird life is most conspicuous during the migration seasons. The Zitting Cisticola (*Bufula tal-Imrewħa - Cisticola juncidis*) and the Sardinian Warbler (*Bufula Sewda – Sylvia melanocephala*) are two resident species that breed here.

Maltese Spurge

Maltese Fleabane

Zitting Cisticola

Sea Squill

Maltese wall Lizard and Moorish Gecko at Mnajdra

THE DISCOVERY

Painting of Ħaġar Qim by Jean Houel (1787)

It is likely that the remains of Ħaġar Qim, which in Maltese translates to 'standing stones' or 'stones of veneration', were never completely buried and remained partly visible even after centuries of disuse. The massive stones protruding in this landscape attracted the curiosity of locals as well as foreign visitors. Amongst the latter was Jean Houel, engraver to King Louis XVI of France whose painting of the site in the 1770s, shows that although the greater part of the site was buried, the larger megaliths were clearly visible protruding through the soil and debris (Houel, 1787, CCLX). Houel's painting even shows two men examining items which they appear to have collected from the ground, a clear indication of the curiosity that the large stone blocks attracted at the time.

The remains triggered the imagination of visitors to the site leading to various theories being proposed in their regard. Abela was the first to document the belief, in the 17th century, that the megalithic temples were built by giants: "*Habbiamo d'avvantaggio alcuni vestige d'opere de'Giganti [...] nel luogo chiamato in Arabico Hagiar el Kim*" (Abela, 1647, pp.145-146).

However, the beginning of the 19th century sees one theory becoming the popularly accepted interpretation of these sites; the belief that these temples were Phoenician in origin. This interpretation of the monuments would last more than a century and is understandable considering the lack

of scientific dating techniques as well as the lack of anything remotely like these sites beyond Maltese shores.

Mnajdra seems to have attracted less attention. The only reference to it prior to excavation in 1840 is by Stefano Zerafa who mentions the site in his study of the geological development of the Islands (Zerafa, 1838, p.xxix). Although this mention is not accompanied by a description, it does indicate that part of the monument was visible prior to excavation.

The First Excavations

The visible megaliths and the curiosity they elicited is what probably led to the early excavation of Ħaġar Qim in 1839, followed by that of Mnajdra in 1840. At the time the only other temple that had been excavated was Ggantija, in 1827, therefore knowledge of these structures was still very limited.

Funds for this excavation were set aside by the Governor of Malta, Sir Henry Bouverie. J.G. Vance, an officer with the Royal Engineers, undertook the supervision of the excavation which lasted three months. Lt. W. Foulis drew up a plan of the site once the excavations were completed. Vance produced a short description of the remains uncovered in the *Malta Times* in 1840 and a more detailed account of the finds and remains in *Archaeologia* two years later.

These accounts give a thorough description of the remains uncovered but do not provide much information on the excavations themselves. Vance says that "nearly all the walls on the northern division bear evident

MALTE

Restes d'un Edifice antique de forme circulaire, à Malte.

Early 19th century engraving of Ħaġar Qim by Demaitre. (Probably after Houel)

marks of the action of fire, some of them, indeed, being quite rotten and having the red appearance of brick" (Vance, 1842, pp.228-229). Vance also observed that the actual material excavated from the site seemed to have accumulated over a long time and that the site had not been buried in one sudden intervention. According to Dr A.A. Caruana, Mnajdra was excavated by Vance in 1840. No information about these excavations exists and Vance only comments on the site saying that "about a quarter of a mile distant from this site (Ħaġar Qim), rather in a hollow than on an eminence, we are enabled to trace the lines of another temple, apparently of a similar form and size" (Vance, 1842, p.232).

The first restoration work at Ħaġar Qim may have been carried out during or just following the first excavation of the site. One of the lithographs by J. Basire, published in 1842 as part of Vance's report, depicts stone pillars supporting a number of broken horizontal slabs. Judging by Basire's drawing and a photograph of the same area published in 1901, these pillars were built in small worked stone blocks.

Lithograph of free-standing 'altar' and decorated slab by J. Basire (Vance, 1842)

The newly uncovered remains drew the attention of scholars from various fields, giving rise to numerous new theories regarding the megalithic temples, especially with regards to their structure, date and origins. In

Lithographs of Ħaġar Qim by J. Basire (Vance, 1842)

1870 Prof. Andrew Leith Adams forwarded a new theory regarding *Mnaidra* and *Hagiar-Kim* in *Notes of a Naturalist in the Nile Valley and Malta*, suggesting that they were close to, or formed part of, an important sea-port town (Adams, 1870, p.241).

At this time the megalithic temples were still believed to be of Phoenician origin, and in 1876 Dr Cesare Vassallo developed this theory and proposed that Ħaġar Qim was dedicated to the seven *Cabiri*, deities originating in the Near East which may have been introduced to the Maltese Islands by the Phoenicians (Vassallo, 1876, p.23-25). He based his theory on the fact that seven statuettes were found within its chambers during the 1839 excavations and the building itself is divided into seven areas. He also suggested that Mnajdra was dedicated to the Phoenician god *Eshmun*.

James Fergusson, who also visited the sites in the 1870s, proposed a chronology for the construction of these two prehistoric monuments. He maintained that at Mnajdra the Middle Temple was the oldest since it had a simpler style, while at Ħaġar Qim the monument first consisted of a single pair of chambers which were then extended by having the inner set of apses converted into a central court (Fergusson, 1872, pp.421-423). He also published calculations made by Colonel Collinson regarding the roof of the buildings saying that this was constructed by means of corbelling and reached a height of around 30 feet.

1885 Excavations

In June 1885 a proposal was made to build a rubble wall around Ħaġar Qim so as to protect it, but as the remains had never been thoroughly surveyed and their extent never actually ascertained, it was decided to carry out further excavation works before the construction of this boundary. Governor Sir John Lintorn Arabin Simmons entrusted Dr A.A. Caruana, who was in charge of the Museum of the Public Library at the time, with the excavations which were carried out between August and December of the same year.

In 1886, Caruana published a report on the excavations together with a proposal for the monument's restoration. The excavations did not yield any new information about the remains but new plans and elevations were drawn by Dr F. Vassallo. In his report Caruana draws up a detailed plan for the restoration of Ħaġar Qim Temples so as to make them "… look almost as complete as when they were originally constructed" (Caruana, 1886, p.1).

Developing a Scientific Approach

Up to the beginning of the 20th century no systematic study was made of the megalithic temples or the finds

VIEW FROM INNER COURT

Drawings of Ħaġar Qim showing the façade of the main building and niche 15, by F. Vassallo (Caruana, 1886)

VIEW OF ORACULAR RECESS

collected during their excavation. A fresh and more systematic approach to the study of these monuments was taken in the beginning of the 20th century by Dr Albert Mayr, a German archaeologist. Mayr conducted a study tour of the Maltese Islands in 1897-98 during which he catalogued all the prehistoric remains known at the time. He published his studies and observations in 1901, providing an extremely detailed description of *Mnaidra* and *Hajiar-Kim* including new plans of the sites. Mayr concluded that the Temples were built before the Phoenician period and possibly dated back to the Bronze Age, between the end of the 3rd and 2nd millennium BC (Mayr, 1908, pp.42-47).

Further excavations at Ħaġar Qim were carried out in November 1909 by Prof. Temi Zammit and Prof. T. Eric Peet. This paved the way for a more extensive investigation at both Ħaġar Qim and Mnajdra in 1910 under the direction of Dr Thomas Ashby, then Director of the British School at Rome. These excavations had two main objectives; to ensure that the plan of the remains had been completely uncovered and to obtain a sample of pottery from each site (Ashby, 1910, 58). They were also the first to record the stratigraphy encountered during excavations.

Trial excavations were made in various apses at Ħaġar Qim bringing to light a number of features within the monuments. Ashby's excavations at Mnajdra led to the discovery of the East Temple, while the area in front of the Central Temple was found to be paved. The Central Temple was also found to rest on an artificial platform, probably built to provide a level surface on which the building could be constructed.

Understanding the Architecture of the Megalithic Temples

Following new information recovered from the 1909-1910 excavations, Zammit published *The Neolithic Temples of Hajar Kim and Mnaidra*

Mnajdra South Temple (Mayr, 1901)

and the "*Miska*" *Reservoirs* in 1927. Here, he proposes a rough date for the construction of the megalithic temples: "We should always bear in mind that we have before us the naked and often mutilated skeleton of the original building, battered and wasted by every adverse agency for six thousand years, so that we can hardly conceive the beauty and the finish of a monument decorated with all the care that an artistically minded people lavished upon it." (Zammit, 1927, pp.11-12)

In the 1930s studies about these sites revolved around the actual structure of the prehistoric buildings and the question of roofing was again placed in the forefront of academic debate. In 1932, Peet suggests that although the apses were most probably covered with a system of corbelling, the central areas were more likely left uncovered (Peet, 1932, p.792).

However, in 1934 Prof. Luigi M. Ugolini in *Malta: origini della civiltà mediterranea* argued that the prehistoric buildings were completely roofed over by a stone vault. He was supported by Arch. Carlo Ceschi who in 1939 published an extensive study on the architecture of the monuments, *Architettura dei templi megalitici di Malta*. He refers to the remains of Ħaġar Qim and Mnajdra Temples in explaining his theories since the remains of corbelling were still preserved in these sites and produces artistic impressions of what the ceiling over the South Temple at Mnajdra would have looked like.

In 1954 further excavations at Ħaġar Qim and Mnajdra by John D. Evans as part of his survey of the prehistoric remains on the islands, revealed the chronology in which the various parts of the temples were constructed. At Ħaġar Qim Evans

Artistic impression of roofing over the South Temple at Mnajdra by Calro Ceschi (1939)

concluded that although the main building went through various phases of construction and renovation, most of these took place in the Ġgantija phase (Evans, 1971, pp.88-90). At Mnajdra Evans concluded that the small trefoil temple was the oldest, dating to the Ġgantija phase, while the South Temple was built in the beginning of the Tarxien phase and the Central Temple was then constructed later on in the Tarxien phase (Evans, 1971, pp.101-103).

This further confirmed the prehistoric origins of the sites, but it was only through the application of carbon dating techniques to the Maltese prehistoric sequence in the 1960s that the Temples of Ħaġar Qim and Mnajdra were unequivocally attributed to the 4th millennium BC.

Giovanni Francesco Abela (1582-1655) was a Maltese of noble birth, born in Valletta to Marco Abela and Bernarda Vella. He became Auditor of Grand Master de Paula, Chaplain and finally Vice Chancellor of the Knights of St. John.

He visited archaeological sites on the islands and made some valuable observations, collecting objects which he thought to be ancient in his country house, the 'Museo di San Giacomo' in Marsa. In the early 17th century he wrote an invaluable work on Malta, 'Malta illustrate con le sue Antichita ed altre Notizie' an important source of information on a number of subjects of Melitensia, such as folklore, place-names, the Maltese language, history, and archaeology.

He is buried in the Chapel of the Blessed Sacrament in St John's Co-Cathedral in Valletta.

Jean-Pierre Houel (1735-1813), a French painter, draughts-man and engraver to King Louis XVI of France. He was born into a family of prosperous artisans and attended the drawing academy in Rouen. In 1769 he joined the French Academy in Rome, where his work was strongly influenced by Italian landscapes, and ancient sites.

He travelled to Sicily, Lipari and Malta between 1776 and 1779 where he painted numerous pictures of the ancient buildings that he visited, each drawing being accompanied by a short description. These were later published as 'Voyage Pittoresque des isles de Sicile, de Lipari et de Malte'.

Antonio Annetto Caruana (1830-1905) was born in Valletta and graduated in Theology. He succeeded Dr Cesare Vassallo as librarian to the Government Public Library in 1880 and was appointed Director of Education in 1887. He was entrusted with the archaeological explorations and preservation of local antiquities from 1880 to 1889. Through co-operation with the superintendent of public works, Caruana discovered, excavated and requisitioned various important archaeological sites including the Roman Domus in Rabat. He was also a member of the first Committee of Management of the Museum in 1903.

Albert Mayr (1868-1924) was born in Passau, Bavaria. He studied Philology at the Ludwig Maximilians University of Munich and was a state school teacher from 1891 to 1917. He visited Malta during autumn and winter of 1897/98 and in spring 1907. He visited the Islands as part of his research for his doctoral thesis which examined the history of the Maltese Islands and Pantelleria until the beginning of the Middle Ages. Between 1894 and 1926 he published ten essays on Maltese archaeology, his major work about the Islands being 'Die Insel im Altertum' published in 1909. Through his systematic studies Mayr reached conclusions which were ahead of the views generally held by scholars of his time.

Thomas Ashby (1874-1931) was a British archaeologist, born to a well-known Quaker family in Staines, Middlesex. In 1902 he enrolled as the first student of the British School at Rome and between 1906 and 1925 was appointed as the third director of the School. As director he not only set a model of research with his pioneering studies of the Roman Campagna, but encouraged as wide a range as possible of students to use the school's facilities, including artists from the Royal Academy and architects from the Royal Institute of British Architects. After his retirement in 1925 Ashby settled in Rome and was elected to a senior research studentship at Christ Church, Oxford in 1930. However, while travelling to Oxford to fulfill the post's residence requirements in 1931, he died tragically when he fell from a train.

Luigi Maria Ugolini (1895-1936) studied at the University of Bologna focusing his thesis on the prehistory of the Bertinoro area. He furthered his studies at the Regia Scuola di Perfezionamento in Rome, carrying out research trips to various Mediterranean countries. In the 1920s Ugolini led a Mission in Albania to locate the Roman towns of Feniki and Butrint. In 1930 Benito Mussolini nominated Ugolini Inspector of Excavations and Archaeological Monuments. In 1934 he published a monograph on Maltese Prehistory and was appointed Professor of Prehistory at the University of Rome.

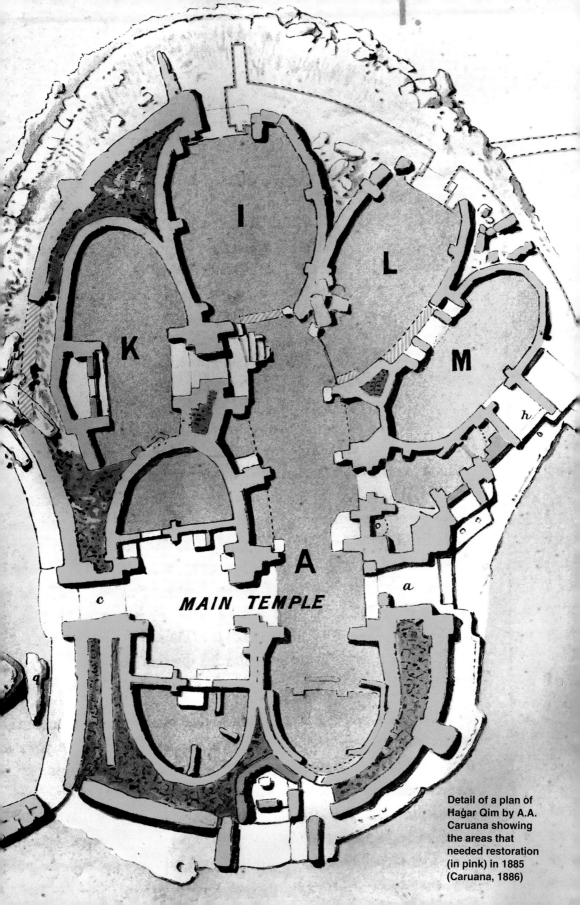

I

L

K

M

h

A

MAIN TEMPLE

c

a

q

Detail of a plan of
Ħaġar Qim by A.A.
Caruana showing
the areas that
needed restoration
(in pink) in 1885
(Caruana, 1886)

THE SITE

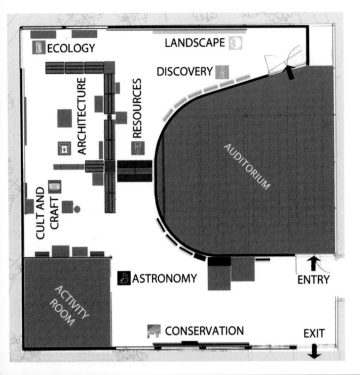

Approaching the site, one must drive through the rugged rural landscape along the south-west coast of Malta. The visitor centre and shelter over Ħaġar Qim are the first that come into view, indicating distinctly the location of this important monument. The sharp lines of the visitor centre contrasts sharply against the natural curving contours of the surrounding landscape. This was designed purposely so as to ensure that a visual distinction is automatically made between the natural and cultural features within the landscape and these modern facilities.

The visitor centre is subdivided into two square blocks distinguishing between the two main functions of this building. The first holds visitor facilities such as ticketing, a cafeteria, souvenir shop and toilets, whilst the

second, accessed over a bridge, holds the exhibition area, dedicated to interpretation and education.

The area dedicated to interpretation introduces the visitor to the textures, sounds, colours, resources, art, landscape, temples and overall mood of Ħaġar Qim and Mnajdra through a 4 minute audio visual presentation. The exhibition is divided into smaller areas dedicated to specific themes related to Maltese prehistory, in particular topics which help in better understanding and appreciating Ħaġar Qim and Mnajdra. Topics include the discovery of Ħaġar Qim and Mnajdra, their landscape context, resources available to the prehistoric community, ecology, temple architecture, pottery making, astronomical alignments and conservation.

'Discovery' presents the discovery, excavation and changing understanding of Ħaġar Qim and Mnajdra from the 17th century to today. This brings the visitor 'face-to-face' with the individuals who brought these sites to light and who through their studies have given us the opportunity to get to know this prehistoric culture. It also provides the visitor with the opportunity to express his/her opinion on the temples.

'Landscape' addresses the question 'Why are the temples here?' and demonstrates how the natural resources, geology, topography, access to the sea and agricultural land have

Interactive information panel in the 'Landscape' section of the visitor centre

Opposite, top: Plan of Visitor Centre, and bottom: Visitor Centre and shelter over Ħaġar Qim Temples

'Discovery' section in the visitor centre

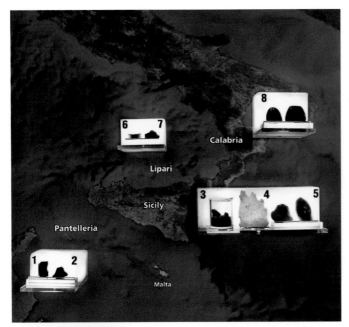

dictated what buildings were built, and what activities took place in the area from prehistory to today.

'Resources' presents the local and foreign resources utilised by people in prehistory and shows the importance that contact with other countries and sea-faring had due to limited local resources. This area also gives the visitor an opportunity to experience at first-hand the properties of different local stones.

'Ecology' purposely provides ample views of the surrounding landscape and draws the visitor's attention to the fact that although this landscape is important for the cultural heritage that it holds, it is also of natural and ecological value. It aims at helping visitors identify and appreciate the flora and fauna they are likely to come across during their visit.

'Architecture' addresses the big question of "How was it possible for people to build these monuments in prehistory?" and visually presents popular theories and possibilities of how this could have been achieved. It also presents the aspect of temple roofing showing how similar roofing techniques were used in more recent years.

'Cult and Craft' focuses mainly on pottery, being the most common type of artefact retrieved in the excavation of these sites. It presents details on pottery making and decorating techniques. This section also points out that we do not know everything

Various materials imported during the Temple Period can be seen in the 'Resources' section of the visitor centre

'Astronomy' section in the visitor centre

about the prehistoric culture and the finds collected from Ħaġar Qim and Mnajdra, and that even the sex of the so called 'fat goddesses' found at these sites is still in debate. A showcase labelled 'mystery objects' gives the visitor a chance to view and hazard an interpretation of some of the objects found at these sites.

'Astronomy' addresses the frequently asked questions about Ħaġar Qim and Mnajdra's alignments to the sun and stars. Through the use of scale models of the temples it also allows the visitor to view solar alignments of the sites all year round.

'Conservation' demonstrates the extent of deterioration suffered by the temples over time. It explains the way natural elements effect the preservation of the sites and why the shelters were necessary to protect them by slowing down the processes leading to their deterioration.

This visitor centre is is fully accessible to wheelchair and pushchair users and is the first on the islands to offer a purposely-built on-site children's activity room. Here

The section about Conservation in the visitor centre demonstrates the extent of deterioration of the temples and why the shelter was necessary to protect them

school groups can hold organised activities during their visits, including role-play and exercises helping them understand various archaeological techniques through active participation. Children visiting the site with parents and guardians can also enjoy a number of fun activities in this room.

Visitors are encouraged to try their hand at all the hands-on activities the centre offers - and why not hazard a visit to the activity room, even if you are not accompanied by a child?

The hands-on display in the 'Architecture' section of the visitor centre

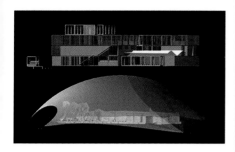

Visitor Centre Design

The Visitor Centre was built in 2008 as part of a project part-funded by the European Union to provide facilities for the 120,000 visitors that come to the sites each year. Its design was chosen through an international design competition launched in 2003 and awarded to Swiss architect Walter Hunziker. It was designed so that it does not break the skyline and horizon when viewed from Ħaġar Qim, meaning any alignment to astronomical phenomena would not be disturbed by the building.

It was located in a pre-existing car park which was larger than the needs of the site, in order to avoid any impact on agricultural land or undiscovered archaeological remains. The building rests on bedrock, constructed in the lowest level to which the bedrock dips naturally to avoid rock-cutting and to keep the building as low as possible. The main floor of the visitor centre has a high ceiling for passive climate control requirements in view of energy consumption and costs – a fundamental design principle that allows it to have a low carbon footprint.

Pot restoration

Amongst the artefacts displayed at the visitor centre is part of a large shallow bowl found at Mnajdra. It is of a coarse unpolished ware and has a notched rim along which is a broad scoop lip.

This is how scholars have known this pot and have been studying it for years. However, during preparations for the exhibition within the visitor centre, Heritage Malta's conservators made a surprising discovery; the pot, which had been put together from various sherds in the past, was actually restored with sherds from two different vessels. Some had even been placed in the wrong positions.

Once the conservators puzzled it out they found that this is what the original pot looked like. This vessel gives us a clear reminder that we will never stop 'discovering' these sites and that some discoveries are made far away from the sites themselves; in this case, in the laboratory of the National Museum of Archaeology.

before

after

Initial designs submitted for the competition launched in 2003.

Overleaf: Interior of Ħaġar Qim (top) and Mnajdra (bottom) Temples

Ħaġar Qim

Aerial view of Ħaġar Qim East Building

Reconstructed stone model of temple façade found at Tarxien Temples, ca. 3250-2500 BC

Ħaġar Qim Main Building façade

Around 100m uphill from the visitor centre one finds Ħaġar Qim commanding views over the surrounding landscape. The site consists of a number of structures; the most extensive and best preserved of these, the main building, is found at the centre of the complex. There are also two smaller outlying ones and the remains of a wall of another structure.

The first building that one approaches at Ħaġar Qim, the East Building, lies in front of the Main Temple and consists of a group of irregular rooms. The use and date of this building are unclear since it does not follow the typical layout of the other temple buildings. One of the rooms is reached through a corridor from the outside and holds two niches or benches.

The main building appears to have been created in a succession of interventions during the 4th millennium BC, resulting in an unusually irregular and complex ground plan. This building may have started off as a four or five-apsed temple, being extended and elaborated over time reflecting ritual and architectural innovations. The walls of this building consist of an external wall constructed in large megaliths, an interior wall of smaller stone blocks, and the space between the two walls being filled with soil and rubble.

The monumental concave façade has become an icon of the Maltese islands. It faces south-east and is approached across an oval forecourt. Part of the forecourt, where there is a natural dip in the rock, was paved in stone slabs, whilst the rest was left unpaved. Particularly noteworthy in the façade are the larger megaliths which are notched in the corners to hold the second course of horizontal blocks, just as in the model found at Tarxien Temples. The entrance, in the middle of the façade, is of the typical trilithon construction consisting of two uprights standing on either side of a threshold and supporting a horizontal lintel. Flanking either side of the entrance

is a stone 'bench' running along the length of the façade. Its function was probably structural helping support the upright megaliths, although it may have had other purposes once in place. In front of the entrance are two interconnected holes cut in the rock floor. Similar holes are often found in front of temple entrances. Their original use is not clear; theories about them range from the possibility that they were libation holes for liquid offerings to their having a technical role in the construction of the doorway.

The entrance leads into a passageway which opens onto an oval area. Within, the two semicircular ends (also known as apses) are screened off from the central area by means of thin stone slabs. Access to these chambers, 2 and 3, is through a so-called 'porthole' slab; a single stone slab that has been pierced in the centre to form an opening. Small notches on either side of these 'portholes' indicate that these doorways were originally closed off by screens or doors. No remains of these were ever found and it is likely that they were made of some organic perishable material such as skins, reeds or wood. Interestingly, the portholes giving access to these apses are not aligned, making it impossible to look into one apse from within the other. A number of architectural elements in the temples appear to dictate visual and at times even physical access in these buildings making it apparent that movement through them and participation in the activities they housed was somewhat restricted.

The floor of the central space, now partly covered by the modern walkway, is paved in stone slabs whilst the floors of the lateral apses are made of *torba*; a lime floor produced

by crushing Globigerina Limestone, spreading it over a rubble foundation, then wetting and pounding it repeatedly to form a hard smooth surface.

During the first excavations of the site in 1839 a stone decorated with a pair of opposed spirals in relief, and a free-standing altar (A) decorated on all four sides with what looks rather like a potted plant or tree in relief were discovered in this central area. These can now be seen at the Visitor Centre and at the National Museum of Archaeology in Valletta respectively. They were moved indoors for conservation purposes and have been replaced on site by replicas. In 1839 five statuettes were

Porthole slabs giving access to the side apses 2 and 3. Note how these are not aligned limiting visual access between these spaces

Overleaf: Aerial view of Ħaġar Qim. Note the trenches excavated in preparation for the shelter

Stone slab (left) and altar discovered in 1839

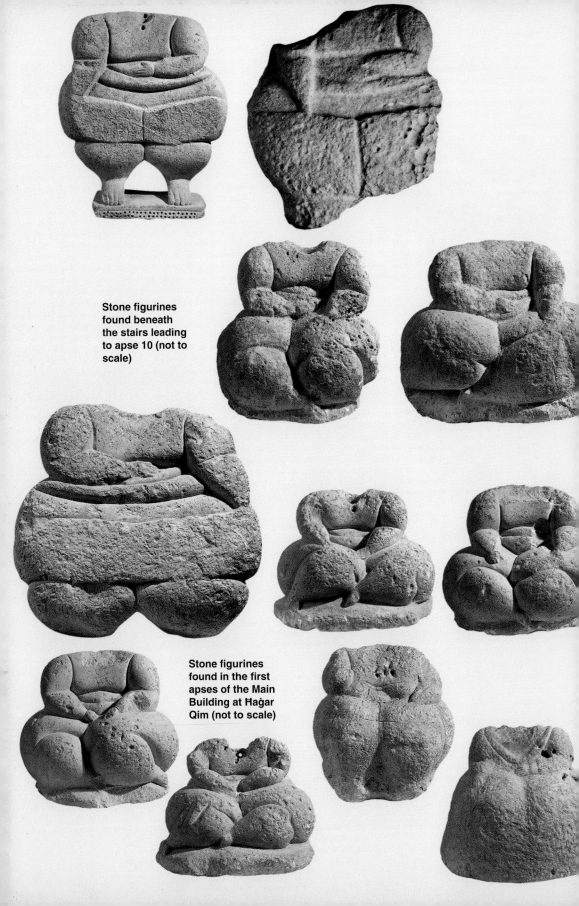

Stone figurines found beneath the stairs leading to apse 10 (not to scale)

Stone figurines found in the first apses of the Main Building at Ħaġar Qim (not to scale)

found close to the altar and another four were excavated from apse 2. In 1909 Sir Temi Zammit discovered a large stone bowl in apse 3; this is also on display at the National Museum of Archaeology.

On either side of the passage leading into the inner chambers of the temple, is a horizontal stone block decorated with shallow holes drilled into its surface. This type of decoration is known as pitted decoration. Beyond the passage, there is an apse to the right, 5, a second entrance from the outside and an oval space to the left, 6. The apse to the right is unusual in that it is closed off by low stone slabs leaving just a narrow opening marked by a stone threshold through which one can access the space inside. Each horizontal course above the walls of this apse protrudes beyond the one beneath forming the remains of the base of a corbelled roof; the type of roof that originally covered parts of these buildings. The elliptical hole at the far end of this apse is of particular significance as it seems to mark the summer solstice sunrise.

The oval space 6 holds three high trilithon altars and the entrances to a number of other chambers. Stone pillars were inserted here shortly after the first excavations in 1839. These were replaced by similar pillars in 1910, but in the 1990s these modern pillars had deteriorated to the extent that further support was required to secure the altars and therefore steel supports were introduced. The altars are now supported by steel supports.

One doorway, flanked on either side by a stone altar hewn out of a single block of stone (B), leads into a small room, 7. Within this room are two smaller spaces or niches, 8 and 9, and what was once a doorway that led outside the building. During the excavation of room 7 in 1839 numerous hemispherical stones were discovered here, and nearly 200 years after their discovery we are still unsure as to their original use or purpose.

Back in the oval area 6, a flight of steps (C) in the southern corner leads up to an elevated room 10. This holds a niche (E) opposite the entrance and an apse within which stands a

Clay figurine found in the first apses of the Main Building at Ħaġar Qim

Large stone bowl found in apse 2 in 1909

Porthole leading to apse 3 with a recess around the opening and notches on either side showing that it was originally covered with a screen or door

Twin seated figurine from the Xagħra Stone Circle, Gozo

Ħaġar Qim apse 10

cylindrical stone pillar (D). The niche is again screened off from the rest of the chamber and is accessed through a small 'porthole' opening. In 1949, during restoration works on the stairs leading to apse 10, three statues and a fragment of a fourth were found buried under the threshold.

Two of the three remaining chambers of the main temple building are also accessible from 6, but this may be partly due to missing or collapsed megaliths and it is likely that their

original principal access was intended to be from outside the building. Stepping through the passage leading outside the temple one immediately notices the blocked doorway on the left leading to the small room 7 mentioned above.

Further west along the external wall of the building is the entrance to the northernmost chamber 11 abutted on either side by two small square niches, 9 and 14. Opposite the entrance to 11 are two small altars. South of this room is another oval chamber 12, with a number of blocks lying on its floor. At the far end of this chamber is a cluster of collapsed megaliths, the study of which might provide us with further information on the original architecture of these buildings.

The last chamber 13 has a gap between the megaliths in its rear wall which gives access to the central oval area 6. In the external wall of this chamber is the relief of two pairs of lower legs and feet (F), recalling the Xagħra twin seated figure. What is unusual about this relief is that it faces into what would have originally been

Relief of two pairs of lower legs and feet in the external wall of apse 13

Below: Central passage of the Main Building at Ħaġar Qim with an entrance at either end

Bottom: Niche 15 on the exterior of the Main Building at Ħaġar Qim

the thickness of the chamber wall. This indicates that either the chamber had a single wall rather than a double wall as is found in the rest of the building, or that it was reutilised and moved here once it no longer fulfilled its original purpose.

Continuing around the exterior of the main building, past the monumental façade, the external wall contains one of the largest megaliths to be used in any temple on the islands. It measures 6.4m in length and 5.2m in height and has been estimated to weigh some 20 tonnes. It would have required a great deal of organisation to raise this megalith, and since it does not appear to have a particular structural function that could not be fulfilled by smaller blocks, it seems to have been placed here primarily as proof of the capabilities of the prehistoric builders.

In the external enclosing wall beside this megalith is a niche (15) that holds a megalithic pillar fronted by a triangular slab. No other temple holds what appears to be such an important feature along its external

View from the North Temple at Ħaġar Qim

Aerial view of the North Temple. Note how only half of this temple has survived

wall. This niche together with other architectural features along the external wall of the main building indicates that, unlike other temples, the external space around the building probably played a role in the rituals and activities it housed. The rear wall of this niche was reconstructed in small ashlar blocks in 1885. Beside this shrine is a small space (16) that gives access to the elliptical hole (H)

in apse 5 which marks the summer solstice sunrise.

Further along the external wall is the highest surviving megalith at Ħaġar Qim, which stands 4.5m high. Curiously, it has a shallow basin cut into its summit. About 30m north of the main temple are the remains of another building; the North Temple. This was originally a four-apsed temple although only its left and central apses have survived. At the far end of this building is a polygonal niche, and to the left of this niche is a stone pillar. To the west of this temple is an irregular group of blocks, the West Remains, which are too disturbed to give any clues as to their original structure, but which again suggest that ritual activities at Ħaġar Qim were not simply concentrated in one main building but radiated outwards into the surrounding buildings and landscape.

Mnajdra

Walking down the paved pathway between Ħaġar Qim and Mnajdra, one can enjoy the relatively untouched landscape between the two sites. Mnajdra comes into view from the edge of the ridge on which Ħaġar Qim was built. From here it is immediately apparent that rather than commanding this landscape like Ħaġar Qim, Mnajdra sits in a natural hollow, blending in as part of it.

Mnajdra Temples consist of three separate buildings accessed across a common forecourt. Various remains are also found to the north-east and south of these buildings indicating that the site may have extended beyond the buildings we see today. The forecourt is paved and has a set of interconnected holes in front of the entrance to the South Temple, similar to the ones found in front of the Main Temple at Ħaġar Qim.

Although the South Temple was built in the Ġgantija Phase, pottery from the earlier Żebbuġ and Mġarr phases found here indicate that the area was in use prior to the

Top: Apse 1 in the South Temple at Mnajdra. Note the entrance to apse 3 on the left

Above: The double-tiered altars in apse 3 (the top altar stone on the right has collapsed)

Right: The threshold of the South Temple at Mnajdra was likely chosen for the crystalline vein running along its length

Opposite left: Wall that collapsed in chamber 5 in 1994

construction of the temples. The concave façade of the South Temple is oriented towards the east and is constructed in a series of vertical megaliths at the foot of which are horizontal stone blocks forming a bench and providing support for the uprights. A trilithon doorway in the centre of the façade holds a threshold which was likely chosen

for the particular dark crystalline vein running along its length. The entrance leads to a paved corridor constructed in four pairs of vertical slabs. The passageway widens towards the interior and holes in the last pair of uprights were probably meant to hold some form of screen or door.

The passage opens onto a large space 1, with an apse on either side. In the apse on the left is a niche covered by a vertical slab, and an elaborate entrance (A) to an inner apse 3. The entrance consists of a porthole entrance set within a trilithon and flanked by two tapered vertical slabs, all of which bear pitted decoration. Considering the elaborate entrance of this apse, it appears to have held particular significance. The small apse beyond this entrance holds two double-tiered altars (B, C).

Opposite the main entrance to the temple is a passage leading from the first apses 1 to the inner ones 2 and 4. This passage is flanked on either side by tapered slabs which are also covered with pitted decoration. These slabs are of particular significance since they were used to mark the summer and winter solstice sunrise. The passage is roofed with stone slabs and a threshold is found between the second pair of uprights. The niche opposite the passage contains a table slab supported on two pillars. The apse to the right, 4 is set at a slightly higher level and the 1910 excavations revealed that this was due to the higher level of the underlying bedrock. During excavations of the floor of this apse a number of roughly-worked clay figurines were discovered.

Back in chamber 1 the northern wall and upper horizontal courses slope inwards to narrow the opening which was originally spanned by a roof. Since four courses have survived here one gets a good idea of what the original roofing might have looked like. In this wall there are two small rectangular openings, one (E) opens onto a recess (6) which is only accessible from the rear of the temple, while the other opens onto a chamber (5) reached up three steps and through a porthole entrance. This chamber holds a niche (D) accessed through a porthole slab also set within a trilithon; the very one that appears

Porthole slab set within a trilithon in chamber 5

Clay figurine and twists of clay discovered in apse 4 during excavations in 1910

on the Maltese 5, 2 and 1 Euro cent coins.

In 1994 heavy rainfall led to the collapse of a wall in chamber 5. This was restored by 1996 but the incident underlined the risk that rain poses to the temples and contributed to the decision to protect the temples with a shelter.

The Central Temple is set on a terrace, at a higher level than the South Temple. Excavations in 1910 and in 1954 revealed that this building was constructed on an artificial platform, formed by piling up stones against the wall of the South Temple to level off the area over which the Central Temple was built.

The main access to this temple is through a large porthole slab, fronted by two upright slabs which form a passage in front of it. Beyond the

Overleaf: Aerial view of Mnajdra

Left bottom: Four upper horizontal courses have survived in apse 1, giving us some idea of what the original roofing looked like

The Central Temple seems to have had two entrances

Engraving of a temple façade on one of the uprights in the Central Temple

porthole slab are two other pairs of uprights continuing the passage into the first apses. To the left of this entrance there seems to have been another doorway. The apses beyond these entrances, 7, are relatively bare, having two horizontal courses supported by upright slabs. The uprights in these apses are smaller than the ones in the South Temple, and their very smooth finish contrasts sharply with the rough external walls.

The taller orthostat (F) to the left of the passage leading to the inner apses carries an engraving of a temple façade. This second passage is paved and opens onto two inner apses 8.

Opposite the passage is a covered niche, while in the left apse is an entrance to a small chamber which was built into the thickness of the temple's wall. The opening to this chamber is similar to the ones in the South Temple consisting of a porthole set within a trilithon arrangement.

The opposite apse demonstrates how the orientation of the megaliths and their resulting exposure to the sun (prior to the installation of the shelters in 2009) has an effect on their deterioration. As a result the megaliths which are south-facing are in a very poor state of preservation when compared to the north-facing megaliths in the same apse.

Just to the east of this temple is a smaller building with a trefoil plan. Its entrance is to the south-west and may have consisted of three doorways or openings. Through the doorways are two wide apses 9, and a smaller one, 10, just opposite the entrance. Apse 10 is closed off by three low stone slabs bearing pitted decoration. Flanking these are two higher megaliths which exhibit particular lines of drilled holes. These holes have been linked to the rising and setting of particular stars

and constellations. The walls of this temple did not survive and were therefore reconstructed in small ashlar blocks in 1952.

The rear exterior walls of the South and Central Temples were built in coralline limestone, readily available in the vicinity of Mnajdra. They were constructed in a 'header and stretcher' technique where megaliths are placed alternately lengthwise along the wall ("stretchers") and with only their short end showing,("headers") to lock into the soil infill across the thickness of the wall adding stability to the whole structure. Sections of this wall now consist of small modern ashlar blocks, the result of reconstructions in the 1950s. At the point where the external walls of the South and Central Temples meet is the entrance to room 6, hidden within the temple walls.

Walking around Ħaġar Qim and Mnajdra, observing their monumental architecture, the manner in which it hides and reveals the spaces within it, and at times determines the actions one has to carry out to access it,

we may just start to appreciate the capabilities of the people who built these sites. The temples proudly attest the resourcefulness and skill of the prehistoric society that created such lasting monumental structures. But the stones we observe today are just an echo of the culture and knowledge that produced these sites. We are still far from understanding the lives of these people, the significance of their temples and the activities that took place within them.

Series of drilled holes on the surface of one of the uprights of the East Temple at Mnajdra. These have been linked to the rising and setting of certain stars and constellations

Central passage and porthole entrance in the Central Temple at Mnajdra

| Solstice JUNE | Mid MAY JULY | Mid APRIL AUGUST | Equinox MARCH SEPTEMBER | Mid FEBRUARY OCTOBER | Mid JANUARY NOVEMBER | Solstice DECEMBER |

Top: Photographic simulation depicting the way in which the rising sun lights the face of the South Temple at Mnajdra throughout the year

Above: The Summer Solstice (left) and Winter Solstice (right) when sunrise lights up the outer edge of the decorated blocks in the South Temple

Incised stone slab from Tal-Qadi Temple depicting what seem to be a crescent and stars divided into sectors

Astronomical alignments

Some finds from the Temples suggest that the people who built them had an interest in astronomy; the movements of the stars, sun and moon. A stone slab found at Tal-Qadi Temple is decorated with eight-pointed stars and a crescent moon, and a potsherd found at Ħaġar Qim carries what looks like a solar wheel.

The strongest evidence for this comes from Mnajdra South Temple where the whole building seems to have been built to mark the sunrise on the Equinoxes and Solstices. At sunrise on the Spring Equinox (21/22 March) and the Autumn Equinox (21/22 September) the two days in the year when the length of day and night are equal, the sun is observed rising in line with the very middle of the doorway. At sunrise on the Winter Solstice (21 December), the shortest day of the year, the sun's rays light the edge of a large decorated slab to the right of the entrance to the inner apses, whilst on the Summer Solstice (22 June), the longest day of the year, the sun's rays light up the edge of a similar slab to the left of the same entrance.

It is not yet clear how this was done but it is likely that rock-cut circular holes such as the one found in the landscape east of Mnajdra may have held posts to record and mark important alignments, during the planning of the temple.

Other indications of an interest in celestial bodies are two megaliths in the East Temple at Mnajdra which may have been used to

Small pottery sherd from Ħaġar Qim decorated with what is popularly called a 'solar wheel'

Solstice, a ray of light enters through an elliptical hole in the wall of apse 5 in the main building. The light is projected as a crescent on a stone slab at the entrance to the apse and as the sun rises higher in the sky, the crescent of light travels down the slab onto the floor and slowly turns into a disk.

The Summer Solstice sunrise creates a particular phenomenon in apse 5 at Ħaġar Qim

mark observations related to the movement of the stars. These megaliths have a series of holes drilled into their surface. F. Ventura, G. Fodera Serio and M. Hoskins suggest that these were a tally of the days between the appearance of one star and another.

Ħaġar Qim is also believed to have its own astronomical alignment. In fact at sunrise on the Summer

The Equinox sunrise as seen from the South Temple at Mnajdra

CONSERVATION OF ḤAĠAR QIM AND MNAJDRA

Following their excavation in 1839-40, Ḥaġar Qim and Mnajdra were exposed to the natural elements, including rain, sun and wind, which gradually wore away the megaliths. Ever since these first excavations concern was expressed for the conservation and restoration of these monuments.

Attempts at preserving and restoring the sites were made by lifting fallen megaliths to their original positions and where necessary, supporting them with modern walls or pillars. One such example is the façade of Ḥaġar Qim where megaliths lying on the ground in front of the façade were placed in their original positions as part of the horizontal courses. This was done in two phases; first in 1910 and then in the 1950s.

In trying to restore the original appearance of the Temples, and in some cases to try to regain lost stability, broken megaliths were repaired using cement, and at times metal dowels. Such repairs were made at these sites as early as 1910, while in 1949, areas of the remains that were considerably deteriorated were "restored" by covering the weathered blocks in cement mixed with Globigerina Limestone chippings. At the time, curators were not aware of the harmful effects that cement has on stone and were in fact acting in accordance with international standards at a time when the *Athens Charter for the Restoration of Historic Monuments* (1931) approved the use of concrete for the consolidation of ancient monuments.

In other instances sections of missing walls were reconstructed in dry-stone walling. This method was first used at Ḥaġar Qim in 1885 and then at Mnajdra in 1910 and the 1950s. These reconstructions can still be seen on site today and while providing an effective representation of the original architecture of the monument they can easily be identified as a recent intervention.

In more recent years, catastrophic incidents such as collapses seem to have increased in frequency and

The façade of Ḥaġar Qim in 1910. Notice how different it looks today following restoration in the 1950s

in intensity, requiring a number of extensive interventions to take place. The most serious collapse in recent times occurred in April 1994, when part of the wall separating the Central Temple from the South Temple at Mnajdra collapsed following heavy rains. Extensive works to restore and consolidate the area of collapse were undertaken and completed by 1996.

Another collapse, this time at Ħaġar Qim, occurred in November 1998 when a wall dividing two apses collapsed. Part of the restoration of this wall, which took place in 2001, involved the introduction of a pillar constructed in well-squared Globigerina Limestone blocks to replace a megalith which had completely disintegrated.

In 2001, a shocking vandal attack took place in four apses at Mnajdra.

During this incident a large number of megaliths were dislodged from their original positions. The restoration of the damaged megaliths carried out in the following months involved the return of the dislodged megaliths to their original locations as well as the repair of damage they sustained during the attack.

When considering these incidents it was gradually realized that reactive measures aimed at reversing damage in specific areas were inadequate to address the sites' problems. It became clear that it was necessary to understand the causes of deterioration and find means for slowing down their effects on the monuments.

In 1999, following an international meeting of experts held in Malta to identify the way forward for the conservation of the Megalithic

Top left: Collapsed wall between apses 3 and 5 at Ħaġar Qim in 1996

Above: Vandal attacks on the sites in 1996 (top), and 2001 (above) also left left their mark on the sites' preservation

RAIN washes away the soil from within the temple walls making them weak and sometimes causing them to collapse. Salts in the stone dissolve when wet.

The **SUN** dries up rain water that seeps into the megaliths and also increases the megalith's temperature. Salts crystallize in the pores in the stone and cause damage.

WIND also dries up the rain water in the megaliths and cools them down, contributing to wet/dry and hot/cold cycles which damage the megaliths. Windblown dust also wears away surfaces.

Continuous wet/dry and hot/cold

Conservation techniques have evolved from the use of traditional rubble walls in the 1950s to the use of the latest design and technology for the construction of a shelter in 2009

Temples, a Scientific Committee was set up specifically to look into the problems of deterioration of the Temples and to recommend solutions. The committee understood that the major risks to the sites are mainly due to environmental factors. These factors have been studied in detail by means of specialized equipment installed on site since 2005.

It was concluded that the sites needed to be protected from direct solar radiation as well as rain, which was identified as the main cause of the collapses that occurred in the 1990s. It was also recognised that our current conservation knowledge does not provide us any safe solutions that can be applied directly on the temples. An indirect measure was

Construction of the shelter at Mnajdra in 2009

therefore necessary to protect the sites from the most serious causes of weathering. This measure also had to be reversible since it is in a way intended to 'buy time' until further research into alternative, and possibly more effective, conservation methods is carried out.

In 2000 the Maltese Government approved the committee's recommendation to protect the temple sites by means of open-sided shelters. The shelters constructed over Ħaġar Qim and Mnajdra in 2008-09:
- protect against solar radiation by directly shading the Temples
- eliminate the effects of water through rainfall, preventing the leaching of infills which could lead to structural instability
- reduce plant growth
- diminish wind impact

Research continues into the deterioration and possible conservation solutions for these monuments, but meanwhile you can help too. As you visit Ħaġar Qim and Mnajdra remember that these sites are very fragile; avoid touching or brushing against megalith surfaces, walk along the routes indicated and if you feel tired during your visit sit on the benches provided. Respect these unique monuments and you too will be helping to preserve these sites for your children to enjoy.

The steel arches that support the protective shelter over Ħaġar Qim Temples

GLOSSARY

Apse: A semi-circular or D-shaped room, often found on either side of a central court or corridor, in the prehistoric temples of Malta.

Carbon dating: A method of dating organic matter by using the amount of Carbon 14 (C14) found in it. All living things maintain a content of C14 in equilibrium with that available in the atmosphere, right up to the moment of death. When an organism dies, the amount of C14 available within it begins to decay a a known constant rate. Comparing the amount of C14 in a dead organism to available levels in the atmosphere, produces an estimate of when that organism died.

Corbelling: A roof constructed using stone slabs that progressively overlap each other to create a vault or dome. The top is finished with a single capstone which spans the remaining hole or is left open.

Eshmun: A Phoenician god of healing and the tutelary god of Sidon. This god was worshipped also in the Phoenician cities of Tyre, Beirut, Cyprus, Sardinia, and in Carthage where the site of Eshmun's temple is now occupied by the chapel of Saint Louis.

Garigue: A low, open scrubland found in limestone sites in the Mediterranean area; characterized by small evergreen shrubs and low trees.

Phoenician: People and objects coming from the area of the modern Lebanon. Used as a period designation, it normally means c. 800-500 BC.

Prehistory: The period of human history before the advent of writing.

Quaternary Period: The period of geologic time starting 1.6 million years ago and continuing to the present day. It is divided into two epochs: the Pleistocene and the Holocene, with the division between these two falling at about 10,000 years before the present. Late Quaternary refers to the time between 700,000 years ago and the present day. It does not necessarily exclude the Holocene epoch.

Solar radiation: Energy that is radiated or transmitted from the sun in the form of waves or rays.

Steppic vegetation: A vast semiarid grass-covered plain, as found in southeast Europe, Siberia, and central North America.

Stratigraphy: A series of archaeological layers that make up an archaeological deposit. Archaeologists use stratigraphy to better understand the processes that created or buried a site over time. Because of natural deposition, soils found deeply buried will have been laid down earlier and therefore are older, than soils found on top of them. Stratigraphic excavation is the digging out of an Area or Site by clearing and recording one layer at a time.

Trefoil: Where three apses open out from a central court, resembling the ace of clubs or a three-lobed leaf.

References:

Abela G.F., 1647, *Della Descrittione di Malta: Isola nel mare Siciliano con le sue antichità, ed alter notitie.* Valletta

Ashby T., 1911, Supplementary Excavations at Hagar Qim and Mnajdra in *Archivum Melitense*, Vol.1 N.2-4, pp.58-60

Ashby T. et.al., 1913, Excavations in 1908-11 in Various Megalithic Buildings in Malta and Gozo, *Papers of the British School at Rome*, vol.6 no.1, pp. 43-109

Caruana A.A., 1886, *Recent Further Excavations of the Megalithic Antiquities of 'Hagiar-Kim' Malta: Executed in the year 1885 under the direction of A.A. Caruana,* Malta

Ceschi C., 1939, *Architettura dei templi megalitici di Malta,* Roma

Evans J.D., 1971, *The Prehistoric Antiquities of the Maltese Islands: A Survey,* London

Fergusson J., 1872, *Rude Stone Monuments in all Countries: Their age and uses,* London

Houel J., 1787, *Voyage Pittoresque des Isles de Sicilie, de Malte et de Lipari.* Paris

Mayr A., 1908, *The Prehistoric Remains of Malta,* Malta

Peet T.E., 1932, The Stone Age Marvels of Malta in *The Wonders of the Past*, Hammerton J.A. (ed.), London, pp. 791-797

Ugolini L.M., 1934, *Malta; Origini della civilta Mediterranea*

Vance J.G., 1840, Hagar Chem or Cham in the Island of Malta: General description of the ruins, in *Malta Times*, 5th October 1840

Vance J.G., 1842, Description of an Ancient Temple near Crendi, Malta, in *Archaeologia*, vol.29, pp.227-240

Vassallo C., 1876, *Dei Monumenti Antichi del Gruppo di Malta.* Stamperia del Governo, Malta

Zammit T., 1927, *The Neolithic Temples of Hajar Kim and Mnaidra and the Miska Reservoirs,* Valletta

Zammit Maempel, 1986, T.A.B. Spratt (1811-1888) and his contribution to Maltese Geology, in *Melita Historica*, 3/9, pp.271-308

Zerafa S., 1838, *Discorso sulla Storia Fisica di Malta e sue Adiacenze*

Further reading:

Cilia D. (ed.), 2004, *Malta before History*, Miranda Publishers, Malta

Gambin K., 2003, *One Hundred Years of Heritage; 1903-2003*, Heritage Books, Malta

Pace A., 2004, *The Hal Saflieni Hypogeum*, Heritage Books, Malta

Pace A., 2006, *The Tarxien Temples*, Heritage Books, Malta

Sultana S., 2006, *The National Museum of Archaeology*, Heritage Books, Malta

Trump D.H., 2005, *Malta Prehistory and Temples*, Midsea Books, Malta

Vella N.C., 2004, *The Prehistoric Temples at Kordin III*, Heritage Books, Malta

Vella N.C., Pessina A., 2005, *L.M. Ugolini; An Italian archaeologist in Malta*, Midsea Books & Heritage Mata, Malta

Vella Gregory I., 2005, *The Human Form in Prehistoric Malta*, Midsea Books, Malta

Zammit V., 2004, *The Limestone Heritage*, Heritage Books, Malta

(Forthcoming) Borg J.J., *A Guide to the Nature Trails of Hagar Qim Archaeological Park*, Heritage Books, Malta